French
REFRESHED

French
REFRESHED

BETTY LOU PHILLIPS

PHOTOGRAPHS BY DAN PIASSICK

GIBBS SMITH

TO ENRICH AND INSPIRE HUMANKIND

Contents

Introduction

Despite the grandeur in which Louis XIV (1643–1715) and his descendants Louis XV (1715–74) and Louis XVI (1774–92) lived in the magnificent Château de Versailles, extravagance rarely suggests elegance these days. Befitting spaces less assumedly scaled than the vast palace, alluring of-the-moment interiors exude a more discreet cachet. Clean, not stuffy, reflects our culture and the times.

As if long overwhelmed by excess, simplicity is the new luxury in the world of design. Both icy formality and ornate are passé. Today's chic settings are sleek, fresh, and brimming with contemporary flair. French leanings are visible—passionate attention to detail, balanced proportions, and kingly artisanship. Quality matters. Fussiness, however, has lost its panache. In rooms worthy of the French, fluid furnishings, cherished accessories, and comfort are in harmony with daily life. Which is to say: More-is-more no longer works. Tellingly, even Paris's most prestigious *grandes dames* that hold coveted French government-certified status—Hôtel de Crillon, Hôtel Ritz, Le Meurice, and Hôtel Plaza Athénée among them—now gleam with pared-down sophistication, a refreshed, less opulent look.

For a while now, designers on both sides of the Atlantic have been hard at work revolutionizing a brand, while social media and design-oriented television programs have helped spread the word to those with aristocratic taste: Lasting respect for the classic past and modern-day spirit rule the decorating world today.

And so, channeling our artistry, energy, and resources in fresh design directions, we confidently fuse comfort and glamour with upscale sensibilities tailored to the demands of twenty-first-century American life. For us, there is no greater pleasure than creating a distinctly French and daringly contemporary haven bathed in style, function, and well-being that meets our needs and works with our everyday lives.

—BETTY LOU PHILLIPS, ASID

OPPOSITE: The French favor layering objets d'art that bring a touch of history to settings. Louis XV consoles (one unseen) with marble tops are from The Gables, Atlanta. Engaging art is central to any room's design.

CLASSIC FRENCH
WITH AN EDGE

*I*mpeccably crafted, regal and grand, eighteenth-century French furniture glorified the reigning monarchs while fueling a taste for splendor among aristocrats across Europe. Whether intent on affirming their wealth and social status with furnishings few others could afford, or fixated on the class divide, the aristocracy effectively ushered unprecedented fame and fortune to France. Paris, in turn, fast became the epicenter of culture, the world hub of the decorative arts.

Notably, scholars worldwide consider the eighteenth century the most elegant era in European history, with French furniture from this period justly singled out for praise. Accordingly, people globally hail the French as icons of artistic authority who knowingly challenged Italy's stylistic might.

It seems entirely appropriate, then, that reverence for eighteenth-century towering armoires, beloved bergère chairs, posh commodes, and noble carpets spans generations. No matter that much has changed in the world since the reign of three Bourbon kings, all named Louis with numerals in ascending order, or that an eon ago most began forsaking regal inlaid furniture with decorative mounts and gilded surfaces for more restrained pieces. Fine French Furnishings continue to exert a pull internationally.

For all its appeal, however, furniture rooted exclusively in the French aristocracy is not necessarily suited to the twenty-first century way of life. And so, with gentrification nudging not only Parisians but also those living in large cities elsewhere, we open the window to a world awash in options, nod to the past, and discreetly push the borders of luxury, whether redefining, reimagining, or refreshing French design.

Layering possessions with classical French lineage that bring immeasurable joy with clean-lined, compelling furnishings that temper the seriousness of everyday life, we aim for a harmonious rather than a homogeneous look that is indeed luxe but far from stuffy. For, clearly, we are in the midst of a movement—not a moment—dispatching the message that savvy design is an expression of personal style and elevated taste, not about envy-inducing opulence steeped in a past era with obvious displays of wealth.

True to this missive, spaces as different as they are alluring say much about our lifestyles, values, and the French people whose discriminating eye and *art de vivre* has earned our admiration and respect.

PREVIOUS PAGE: A home with modern luxuries is rooted in tradition. Standing ready to welcome guests: a soaring entry with towering ceiling, dramatic stone stairs, and walls warmed with Venetian plaster, omnipresent in Paris. First used in Italy during the Renaissance, the technique borrows alluring tints such as dove, ivory, and champagne from luminous 18th-century silks. The bronze and crystal chandelier, from Jean-Pierre Carpentier Antiquités in the famed Marché aux Puces de Saint-Ouen, once hung in the renowned London hotel Claridge's.

An admirably crafted P.E. Guerin lockset exudes artisan details. The New York–based company, founded in 1864 by Frenchman Pierre Emmanuel Guerin, reportedly boasts a client list that rivals Marquis' *Who's Who*.

ABOVE: Art collected over time lines the gallery walls. Custom Montecito lanterns are by Formations; easily maintained stone flooring from Paris Ceramics.

OPPOSITE: Classical elegance and modern allure meet on an Ebanista Louis XVI settee, with exquisite carving layered with gilding.

LEFT: An arched opening frames a salon with *parquet de Versailles* flooring and an Ebanista area rug, handmade in Afghanistan. Together they lay the groundwork for furnishings, palette, and textures to play a strong role. Crystal chandeliers, circa 1880, are from Jean-Pierre Carpentier Antiquités in Saint-Ouen, north Paris. Floor-to-ceiling window treatments wear textured Thai silk from Bangkok-based Jim Thompson. Seating floats in the space rather than stiffly hugging the perimeter of the room, making conversing easier and the large room feel more inviting.

ABOVE: A bouquet of tightly bundled peonies—in full bloom and straight from the garden—showers the salon with color. Although French artist Édouard Manet (1832–83) is best known for painting everyday life—with its beggars, prostitutes, and *bourgeoisie*—peonies cut from his family's Gennevilliers garden in 1864-65 became a source of inspiration.

ABOVE: Inherited or not, we admire the beauty of a circa 1750 Louis XV walnut commode and value its practicality for storing linens.

OPPOSITE: Swathed in Venetian plaster, a salon reads elegant, not at all stuffy. The works of French artists Édouard Cortès, Jules-René Hervé and Eugène Galien-Laloue (signed under the pseudonym J. Liévin) preside over the 17th-century carved-stone mantel from Ancient Surfaces, NYC. Large canvas framed in gimp is from Le Louvre French Antiques, Dallas. Italian crafted Buccellati picture frames merit a place on the 18th-century commode from Jacqueline Adams Antiques, Atlanta. Loveseats wear Cowtan & Tout and flaunt channel tufting.

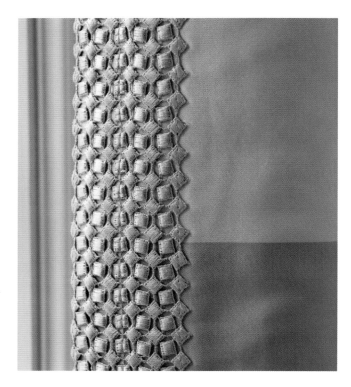

THIS PAGE: Details matter. Whether a Houlès trim delivers luster to a window treatment, tufts add pizazz to a loveseat, or embroidery embellishes an Etamine sofa pillow, an eye-catching finishing touch has the potential to make the ordinary extraordinary.

OPPOSITE: A head-turning armoire that withstood the bedlam of 18th-century France is a backdrop for flawlessly tailored upholstery perfectly scaled to the size of the salon. Fabric from Christopher Hyland, woven in France, covers the sofa, while Coraggio Textiles adorns glazed chairs-and-a-half. The coffee table introduces a dash of modernism into the traditional setting.

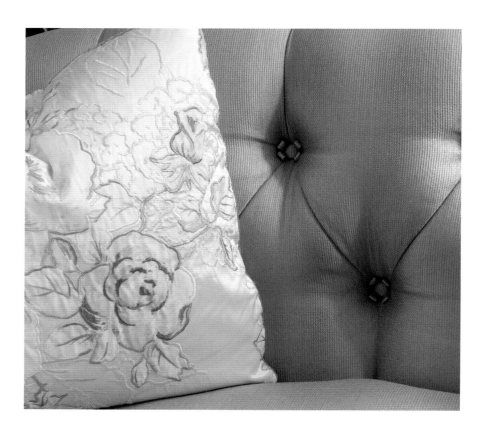

LEFT: A wine wall projects a fresh, modern sensibility, while textured Giardini Wallcovering, produced in Milan, encircles the room. Casamance covers chairs surrounding the custom Gregorius Pineo dining table. Marcie Bronkar's "Tea Leaf" fabric flows from iron rods. William Yeoward hand-cut crystal "Beehive" centerpiece and candlesticks from Bergdorf Goodman, NYC, look up to Baccarat pendants. In France, hours-long, multicourse dinners often include wines as special as the food.

ABOVE: An oil on canvas of epic proportions (approximately 8 x 6 feet) touts its original gilt frame lauding the painting's honorable mention at the 1923 Paris Salon. Signed C. Buffin (1871–1926), *La Foire St. Christophe à Tourcoing* centers on a fair in the square near St. Christophe Cathedral in the village of Tourcoing, on the Belgian border in northern France. Vintage meat trolley is from Bergdorf Goodman.

ABOVE: The exquisite craftsmanship of Sherle Wagner International—a premier source for luxury hardware—has attracted eyes worldwide since its founding in 1945.

OPPOSITE: Wallpaper by Rubelli is in step with the times, while in an earlier era fabric would have swaddled the walls in a French powder room. White onyx pedestal sink and rock crystal fittings are by Sherle Wagner. The Bright Group sconces and John Gregory pendant light the setting.

OPPOSITE: Like others on the best-dressed list, these impeccably attired countertops wear Calacatta Gold marble from Architectural Granite & Marble, Austin. Three oversized Gregorius Pineo pendants (one unseen) illuminate the freestanding, 14 x 5–foot island central to the kitchen's presence. Working together, an Élitis sheer and Samuel & Sons trim diffuse the morning light. Television is on an undulating arm. Range hood is bespoke.

LEFT: Playful yet refined, Christofle's "Mood"–a streamlined, contemporary egg that holds flatware service for six—is a staple in many kitchens.

RIGHT: Undeniably chic: Villeroy & Boch's "NewWave" snack set and Artistic Frame's undercounter stools. A China Seas linen with scattered, diminutive dots covers the latter.

PREVIOUS OVERLEAF: Disparate eras working together in an asymmetrical, inviting way convey a modern air (whereas traditional interiors favor symmetry or mirror imagery). In a family and friend friendly room, where brown tones vary, pattern and texture play a key role in increasing the feeling of depth as the eye surveys the space. Knit backing helps stabilize the fabrics, thus preventing the

Rogers & Goffigon linen on sofas and Texture paisley and Hodsoll McKenzie print on swivel chairs from stretching. Eighteenth-century mantel is from Pittet Architecturals, Dallas. Valencia chandelier is by Paul Ferrante.

ABOVE: Stripes are chic, whether run horizontally for a modern edge or vertically in the traditional manner. Fabric on windows is from Christopher Hyland. Even

in neutral territory, a hint of color works. Distinctive Scalamandré sheathes the chair faces, while embroidery from Old World Weavers envelopes the backs. Game table is old. Hermès playing cards are immediately recognizable by their orange box and horse-drawn carriage logo.

OPPOSITE: Scalamandré on front juxtaposed with Old World Weavers embroidery on back.

LEFT: Top-tacked Christopher Hyland window treatment plunges from ceiling to floor, exalting simplicity, while an 18th-century walnut corner cupboard from Jacqueline Adams Antiques speaks of a rich past. Serious cooks on both sides of the Atlantic prize copper cookware.

RIGHT: Whether dining with family or friends, mixing harmonious, disparate patterns—such as Ralph Lauren "Côte d'Azur" salad plates and "Mason" dinner plates with Christofle flatware and Kate Spade tumblers—creates a sense of occasion. Matchy-matchy is out of fashion when it comes to setting the mood. Bountiful fresh flower arrangement is from Ken Miesner's Flowers, Ladue, Missouri.

OPPOSITE: In high style, the breakfast room's reclaimed beams spark interest, while dining in the round makes conversing easy. Bursts of blooms mingle with furnishings from Gregorius Pineo and fabrics from Old World Weavers (chair pads), Rodolph (ties) and Dedar (curtains), an Italian mill. Mantel is old. Iron Age, Dallas, fabricated the curved rod, working from a template sent from St. Louis contractor Jim Minton.

ABOVE: In Parisian powder rooms, color is a rarity, whereas on this side of the Atlantic, a powder room mirror is not simply a mirror but rather a canvas to display reflected art. Here, an Hermès scarf framed in Lucite is the accessory of choice. Unassuming Bright Group sconces and Hartmann & Forbes wallpaper add to the ambiance.

OPPOSITE: Though tucked beneath a staircase, the area makes a definitive style statement. Impeccably dressed 19th-century children's chairs (wearing a Sanderson check) and midcentury coffee table were unearthed at Country French Interiors, Dallas. Print on sofa is from fifth-generation, Venezia-based Rubelli. Projecting a trace of playfulness is the leopard patterned stair runner from Stark Carpet.

OPPOSITE: Her envy-inducing home office exudes a worldly air. Striking black-and-white photographs by Joani White include Buckingham Palace mounted in three panels to accommodate a curved wall. Photos of the Eiffel Tower hang elsewhere in the room. Curved sofa wears an oversized Sanderson pattern edged in Zoffany tape. Nesting tables and bar cart are vintage. Custom area rug in the round is from Stark Carpet.

LEFT: Behavioral psychologists say we each need a personal space to do what we love or what needs to be done. Generous windows frame enviable views, making work-related tasks significantly more pleasant. Eames chairs from Design Within Reach—with pneumatic lift—give the space a modern spin, while desk accessories from Ellis Hill, Dallas, help keep the area organized. Lamps are Baccarat, established in 1765 in a small village with the same name. Throw is by D. Porthault, the ninety-some-year-old purveyor of fine French linens and more.

RIGHT: An unapologetically feminine workplace pays homage to the timeless appeal of Coco Chanel's favorite color—black. High-gloss cabinets offer ample storage space and are sufficiently deep to house a printer and other work-related supplies. Wallpaper is by Maya Romanoff.

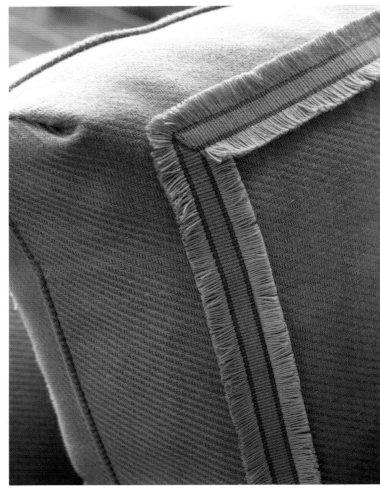

LEFT: Custom 90-inch-tall John Rosselli lantern seizes the opportunity to become the center of attention. These days, wattage no longer measures bulb brightness. Instead, lumen is the new watchword, with packaging fact sheets comparing lumens to watts and indicating color.

RIGHT: A Holland & Sherry trim teams with Holland & Sherry earth-tone fabric to tailor the look of His comfort zone.

OPPOSITE: Resplendent walnut paneling lines the two-story bookshelves on opposite sides of His study, as if taking German novelist Heinrich Mann's (1871–1950) words to heart: "A house without books is like a room without windows." Tucked among the shelves are a wealth of hardback and paperback books along with reminders of favorite moments in time.

ABOVE: The centuries-old, open-air bookstalls hovered along the banks of the River Seine are fighting for survival, yet, in 2017, the French reportedly bought nearly twice as many printed books per capita as Americans. Leather pulls are from Turnstyle Designs, England.

RIGHT: For a dedicated reading area, admirable artisanship went to extremes. The walnut coffee table with built-in storage changes the look of the made-to-order ottoman. Handwoven leather area rug is from Holland & Sherry.

OPPOSITE: A covetable 17th-century *cheminée* from Antique Surfaces imbues this master bedroom with more than a bit of French sensibility. Chairs wear Zimmer + Rhode embroidered circles, rich in symbolism. Ottoman hosts durable GH Leather—in sync with the relaxed spirit of the home.

LEFT: Various shades of blue create a serene master, after a move prompted a Patina bed to transition from *chocolat,* with help from Sanders Studio, Dallas. Layered lighting includes a Marseille rock crystal chandelier from Niermann Weeks, bedside lamps from Allan Knight, and light from the fireplace. A Clarence House damask covers the 19th-century Louis XVI bench. Windows wear Zimmer + Rhode, lined and interlined, offering both privacy and protection from the sun.

RIGHT: In Her fashion-forward closet, a glamorous Murano pendant dazzles. The difference between a chandelier and a pendant? Both suspend from the ceiling on a chain or cord; however, a pendant hangs directly down from a single chain, while the multiple arms or candelabra sleeves of a chandelier branch up and out, with each arm holding a bulb.

ABOVE: With a place for everything and everything in its proper place, His most humble clothing staples reside unseen, in drawers.

RIGHT: The homeowners each have their own customized closet, with His reflecting the disposition of a well-organized man. The space includes a rack for belts, an island for packing, and a window seat for putting on his shoes. A tie rack is unseen.

OPPOSITE: Complementing nature's beauty is a durable sink from Vermont Soapstone that is impervious to chemicals and heat. When fresh from the quarry, the nonporous stone is light gray. Exposure to water, grease, and oil results in a rich charcoal color. Bringing the outside in, Phillip Jeffries wallcovering helps take the drudgery out of washday.

ABOVE: Fern-filled stone planters flank the laundry sink. Statement-making arced faucet with pull-out spray is by Grohe.

LEFT: When company calls, a sanctuary with African undertones stands ready. The wallpaper and the suede bed skirt fabric are both from family-owned Pierre Frey. GH Leather, Houston, sheaths custom, button-tufted headboard with nailhead trim. Sham and coverlet fabric is by Rogers & Goffigon. Richard Wrightman, NYC, crafted the luggage racks and folding bar table that serves as a night table. Mismatched night tables make the room more interesting. Area rug was handwoven in India for Marc Phillips, NYC.

ABOVE: Tucked in a corner is a comfort zone perfect for reading. Chair and ottoman, upholstered by Marroquin Upholstery, Dallas, in Schumacher linen, and D. Porthault throw amp up the setting's neutral tones. Roman shades sport Maria Flora. Photography by Joani White brings a dash of the wild to the space.

LEFT: Brush fringe and flange with Turkish corners—impossible to ignore—bring unexpected dimension to the silhouettes of a chair and ottoman. Diverse textures can also soothe the way to the feeling of well-being by softening hard edges and delivering warmth.

RIGHT: Leather binding joins forces with a runner from Patterson Flynn Martin, Schumacher's sister company, to make a design statement on stairs leading to an upper floor. In France, the second floor is a most private space.

OPPOSITE: Schumacher's navy grass cloth wallcovering paired with thoughtful amenities—including a standby toothbrush, toothpaste, phone charger and Wi-Fi password—make a welcomed guest feel pampered.

PREVIOUS OVERLAY: The epitome of chic: Embroidered bed linens from Schweitzer nestle on admirably crafted, custom four-poster bed from Thomas Love, Arlington, TX, who also crafted the room's chest and desk. Far from an afterthought was the commissioned oil on canvas depicting the noble city of Venice (after the flood) by Susie Pryor. Hydrangeas complement the Kravet blue check on lampshades.

OPPOSITE: To preserve natural light, Scalamandré fabric extends beyond the width of the window, with no skimping on fabric. For très chic richness, workrooms ceremoniously calculate fabric at two-and-a-half—and more often than not—three-times the length of the curtain rod, including returns. Bergère chairs, rooted in the era of Louis XV, mix with modern ottoman and drink table—a practical addition—offsetting traditional lines. Underfoot, a graphic patterned area rug from Patterson Flynn Martin.

ABOVE: Upon the desk sits a hollow, handblown Venetian glass lamp from Donghia. Fabric on shade is from Kravet, and on chair from Jim Thompson. The finishes deliver warmth to the room.

ABOVE: A sumptuous en suite bathroom, wallpapered in Phillip Jeffries, hosts a freestanding Empire tub with roll top—a style adapted from a look popular in England and France during the late 19th century. Like all 90 x 90-centimeter Hermès silk scarves, the framed street scene tells a story. Towels are Matouk. Sconces are damp-rated, as should be all fixtures in bathrooms.

OPPOSITE: A room with modernist allure boasts all the essentials: a guest-worthy Royal-Pedic mattress, Donghia bedside lamps for reading, a desk (unseen) on which to place one's laptop, plus a chair and ottoman. And, naturally, freshly laundered and pressed bed linens. Sheets are from Yves deLorme, as is the cashmere throw. Europeans tend to lay their pillows flat and cover them with the coverlet, while those living in the States are more apt to prop them vertically against the headboard. The pitched ceiling influenced the headboard's height, and the window casing impacted its width. Roman shades are Romo. "Peonies along the Garden Wall," an ink-and-acrylic on canvas by Carlos Ramirez, is a joy to view.

OPPOSITE: Defined by stainless steel glass-front cabinets, a catering kitchen worthy of the title makes entertaining easy. With a matchless mix of practicality—ample storage—and pizazz—lengthy expanses of Calacatta Gold marble—it is the go-to area for both formal and informal parties.

ABOVE: With everything in plain sight, organization is a must.

BELOW: A gallery hosts the best of two worlds: a vintage French pastry table and contemporary art. *Bird's Nest* is by Susie Pryor and *Silenced* by Bruce Brainard. Pryor Fine Arts in Atlanta represents both artists.

ABOVE: A reclaimed oak pocket door, circa 1880–1900, boosts the profile of the wine room entrance. Hardware is from Rocky Mountain Hardware.

OPPOSITE: Stone walls frame an intimate tasting room complete with 19th-century walnut table and embossed leather chairs from Le Louvre French Antiques. Pittet Architecturals transported both the reclaimed tile flooring and firebrick on the curved, groin vault ceiling from France. The oversized chalkboard was moved from the owner's former home.

ABOVE: A pretty ribbon is a gift's best friend.

OPPOSITE: Modest or palatial, a wrapping room is a coveted amenity. Here, Manuel Canovas "La Parisienne" wraps the walls.

OPPOSITE: Humble teak paired with graphic York wallcovering lines the walls and transitions onto the ceiling, splashing a pool bath with style. Blue-and-white-striped towels with yellow tassels are by Serena & Lilly.

ABOVE: Vertical patterned wallpaper softens angles, making the bath appear larger and walls taller in a room with a pitched ceiling. The window basks in terrycloth from Old World Weavers and Samuel & Sons trim. Framed or unframed, a Hermès scarf is a work of art.

OPPOSITE: Come summer, the bar-height table and chairs from Michael Taylor Designs become a destination spot for dining *en plein air,* while market umbrellas from Santa Barbara Designs offer protection from the sun. With every pool needing an element of playfulness, Wendy Williams Watt's inflatable "love" balls, whether five-foot, three-foot, or one-foot, are meant to send a global message of inclusivity.

ABOVE: Amanda Lindroth toss-away place mats and bite-size Juliska melamine plates work for spur-of-the-moment dining on the lanai. Tumblers are from Mario Luca.

ABOVE: Eschewing formality, an old-world, built-in pizza oven—complete with Kalamazoo tools—stands ready to host a crowd, with help from an unseen grill. Unabashedly modest Brazilian soapstone lines the countertop.

OPPOSITE: A lanai as style-savvy and welcoming as an indoor room brings relaxed sophistication. (Retractable screens vanish with the flip of a switch.) Stain-resistant Maria Flora solids and stripes smartly outfit Michael Taylor Designs' "Montecito" collection. A Serena & Lily area rug anchors the seating group. Indoor-outdoor lamps are from Arteriors.

MIXING ERAS
AND AESTHETICS

*F*amous for their discerning eye and predilection for stylish living, the French consider the legacy of design—unparalleled craftsmanship, enviable artistry, and innate flair—a birthright, a gift inherited if not intuitive. No matter that rooms dripping in baroque splendor failed to hold lasting appeal. Or that cold postwar minimalism—once de rigueur in many fashionable mid-twentieth-century addresses—also failed to strike the right stylistic note.

These days, design cognoscenti rarely strive for period authenticity any more than appear preoccupied by the past. Armed with educated eyes, unerring tastes, and unrivaled confidence, most have moved on. Weaving furnishings befitting the moment among classics rich in meaning, they appear intent on honing the style of a new generation coming of age if not inspiring an international audience.

Leaving nothing to chance, the French play an ongoing role in shaping and reshaping the stylistic world. For them, design is as much an expression of values and viewpoints as it is an aesthetic statement. In an age filled with options, where it is easy to become overwhelmed by choices, the savvy underscore their influence by purposefully spreading the word that nothing quite rivals quality as the hallmark of the quintessentially French room, regardless of artistic inclinations having shifted.

And we get the point. Quality is paramount. Long touted as the secret to lasting beauty, quality raises the bar on luxury. With splendor in astonishingly handsome wood pieces with deep carving, tongue-and-groove joints, and the patina of age and comfort hidden in durable, kiln-dried hardwood frames and eight-way hand-tied springs of sofas and chairs, our mind-set prompts us to do as the French do. We aim for legs as a continuation of the frame and joints doweled with thick wooden pins rather than simply screwed into the frame, which tends to make them squeak and split over time. Though it is hard to resist a bargain, we snub temptation and instead buy the best we can manage, aware that uncompromising standards result in some furnishings being more expensive than others. What's more, settling for second best can equate to a pricey lesson when an affordable alternative begets short-lived joy.

We are partial to furnishings that come with a backstory. Ultimately, the point of pride confirming value and status is provenance. Indeed, we are the first to admit that an interesting history, such as surviving the French Revolution or a World War, adds allure, though to some it hardly matters if the document itself has long since disappeared. Most important is passion for the piece and its distinctiveness.

This is to say that design aficionados are unwilling to settle for any room lacking imagination, or worse, looking commonplace. Taking our cue from the French, purchasing matchy-matchy bedroom furnishings (bed, nightstands, chest, and dresser) or a dining room "set" (table and chairs) with wood finishes uninterestingly alike isn't our style. Dissimilar yet harmonious is. As for lighting, we like it to bring drama into the setting. Accordingly, we also frown on five-piece place settings of the same china. With heightened awareness influencing our views, disparate elements come together in a fluid way with more than a modicum of success.

Invariably, then, our settings have an edge, which is not to imply they are overly decorated, but rather, are distinctive anthologies of sorts—with diverse furnishings and compelling accessories testifying to impeccably informed tastes.

PREVIOUS OVERLEAF: A 19th-century Louis XV marble-topped console and a mirror from the same period grace this entry. Long-lasting cymbidiums integrated into the floral arrangement by Dallasite Logan Jones ensure that this entry looks its best.

Black and white makes a strong statement. In the Île-de-France—the historic heart and most populous hub of the country encompassing Paris and surrounding seven *départements*—one seldom sees bold color on walls or upholstery. Here, a romantic palette is the framework for tasteful living. Sofa fabric is by Great Plains. Slipper chair with nailhead trim is custom. The midcentury coffee table from Jan Showers hosts an arrangement by Logan Jones. Edgy art—an acrylic using Sumi ink—is by Raymond Saá, professor of art at Drew University.

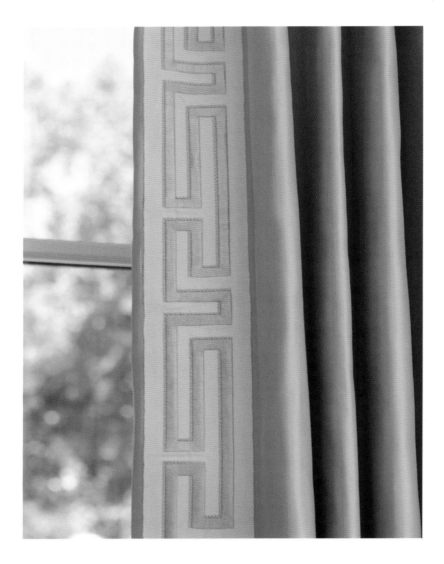

ABOVE: Adorning the leading edge of the window treatment is the Greek key. The motif took its name from the Maeander River in ancient Greece (now Turkey), whose irregular path symbolizes infinity.

RIGHT: Mingling lavender with neutrals delivers a level of sophistication difficult to obtain when introducing a decidedly saturated hue. Windows wear Romo fabric and Houlès trim. In keeping with the French less-is-more philosophy, which teaches that one liberally scaled treasure can have a greater impact than the Paris Métro full of antiques, the carved, pink marble leaf on the coffee table is a conversation starter. Seemingly, most French think like Napoléon (1769–1821), who told his followers, "Everything that is big is beautiful."

PREVIOUS OVERLEAF: In a dining room awash with color, texture, and drama, a pleasing mix of French and American influences bridges the gap between two cultures. Salvaged 18th-century polychrome paneling, inset with mirrors from the 1920s that once wrapped the walls of a Parisian *appartement*, visually widen the space. Henredon oval table has been in the family for nearly forty years; the chairs even longer. Chandelier from the fifties is original to the house.

ABOVE: Hotel silver tray from Paris's revered Hôtel Athénée holds a beverage server, tumblers, and goblets. A tablescape with a variety of heights, textures, and shapes makes an artful display.

ABOVE: In their vibrant glory, mini cymbidium orchids add energy to the palette.

LEFT: Samuel & Sons trim draws attention to the Zimmer + Rhode top-tacked window treatment secured with rings happened upon at the Paris Flea Market.

OPPOSITE: Whether set in France or in the States, practicalities such as admirable linen hand towels and an attention-grabbing antique mirror exude unmistakable style. Console is custom. Faucet and towel bar are from Herbeau.

ABOVE: In 18th-century France, the ante–powder room was an ideal spot for powdering one's wig. Today this chic space is equally useful for catching one's breath or sharing secrets. Silver is a family heirloom. Painterly periwinkle wallcovering from Great Plains is fresh yet sophisticated.

Following a devastating fire, a whirlwind makeover transformed this kitchen, breakfast room, and unseen sitting area into a bright, sumptuous area. Countertops are Calacatta Blue polished stone from KLZ Stone Supply.

LEFT: A grocery bag rarely prompts admiration; however, Ellis Hill, Dallas, is awash in inspiration with its monogrammed linens, Murano goblets, and enticing stationery. Then, too, the rue de Turenne, in the Marais, is a tabletop nirvana.

RIGHT: An unexpected dash of color adds warmth to a neutral setting, thanks to the pincushion protea that floral stylist Logan Jones designed as centerpiece. Surrounding a Knoll table are chairs slipcovered in "Mist," a washable quilted fabric from Savel Textiles. Frog closures are custom.

OPPOSITE: Designed for coffee aficionados, a bar boasts French presses by Bodum sans paper filters, which absorb natural oils.

ABOVE: A fashionable home deserves a fashion-forward laundry room to take the drudgery out of washday.

OPPOSITE: A lotus-patterned wallcovering from Galbraith & Paul puts a playful spin on a powder room flooded with light. Wooden carved-leaf mirror is from Jan Showers.

ABOVE LEFT: When pastels reign, an unpretentious throw can bestow warmth. Striking Murano amethyst lamp is from Jan Showers. Curtains hang from custom acrylic rods.

ABOVE RIGHT: The influence of Louis XVI (circa 1850 desk and circa 1890 fauteuil robed in Stark and Osborne & Little fabrics) is clear. Mixed media on paper are by Dallasite Corinne Bizzle,

represented by Park and Eighth in Fort Worth.

BELOW RIGHT: Passion for mixing minerals and metal led Dallas artisan Larry Whitely to create this luxurious rock crystal flower sculpture.

OPPOSITE: Layered in serenity, a luxe master bedroom has more than a modicum of presence. Handwoven area rug is from Stark Carpet, bedding by Peacock Alley, and convex round mirror from Ceylon et Cie. In keeping with the soothing palette, the sofa wears Donghia fabric and throw pillows are covered in Designer's Guild. Chandelier is Antiques Moderne.

LIVING ARTFULLY

The country credited with inventing *haute couture* as well as bringing the *atelier* out of the Middle Ages has long revered the meticulous skills of highly accomplished artisans who wield a needle, lathe, or other tool of the trade—some using centuries-old techniques. Whereas the enduring appeal of excellence remains a source of fierce national pride, French interest in excess has waned.

Scorning centuries of conformity, opulent interiors swathed in extravagant furnishings no longer satisfy the unassuming penchant of modern-day sophisticates. With livability and restraint the guiding spirits, clean lines, streamlined silhouettes, and contemporary artwork are redefining luxury for current tastes.

Whether updating an *appartement* in the heart of Paris or a getaway in Saint-Jean-Cap-Ferrat overlooking the Mediterranean Sea, having a clear vision, comprehensive plan, and keen eye are central to creating a setting that radiates beauty, comfort, and the feeling of well-being. But, then, ingenuity helps, too.

Yet even those French with confidence to spare will admit that shifting creative direction is not always easy. Although some solutions come quickly, many do not. What's more, inspiration does not always come from within. They happen upon it in their travels, during excursions to museums and the theater, on fashion runways and, quite naturally, in the design industry itself.

This is not to suggest that their everyday world fails to prompt new ideas, nor to imply that all visions are attainable. Some thoughts demand compromise and certainly others are out of reach.

It is safe to say, transforming a room can prove challenging. Paring down requires determining which pieces are going to work and necessitates editing others—at times, far from subtly. With or without undertaking a major overhaul, a minimalistic mind-set can entail parting with more than a few family heirlooms in the process. There are exceptions, of course, but at times, memories can be difficult to let go.

Trusting their instincts more often than a decorator to achieve individual visions, the French begin reworking a site by building around a treasured wood piece (or two) that makes a strong case for its presence. Thinking imaginatively, they then meld styles—merging contemporary furnishings with earlier influences while keeping in mind that some furnishings simply are not meant to share a setting. Beyond that, those that are meant to share a setting need breathing space to be appreciated. Ultimately, design is a balancing act. With neither symmetry nor mirror imagery dictating furniture placement, the most inviting areas are often awash in furniture set on an angle, floating in space, thus opening up the room and perhaps, above all, resulting in a sense of ease.

In French minds, harmony is more important than conforming to past ideals. Added to that, an artfully assembled collection is fundamental to elevating a room to surprising heights. Mismatched or not, collections look best when grouped together, not scattered around the room. Teaming the understated with that more grand reflects French schooling. Slices of geodes or sculptural objects that emit light, or prized candlesticks varying in height can give unexpected life to a mantel while delivering glamour to a room.

With education lying somewhere near the very heart of French cultural identity, books offer insight into interests while exuding valued evidence of literary minds.

PREVIOUS OVERLEAF: A hand-forged wrought iron door—understated yet grand—befits the exterior façade of a château in which modern references abound.

OPPOSITE: Black and white marble and hand-forged wrought iron unite to create a dramatic vaulted foyer with contemporary polish. Working together, esteemed Dallas architect Richard Drummond Davis and interior designer Deborah Walker fashioned the space. Iron Age fabricated the railing.

Bolstered by knowledge, most view the scholarly air of *la bibliothèque,* or home library, as an extension of self. For their part, far-reaching views of the world and opinions about a broad array of issues readily articulated empower the French with confidence. To that end, grouping books by subject matter works, but categorizing by color or giving the illusion of appearing staged, not at all. Whether propped vertically or horizontally, it would be unusual to see spines covered in white paper in a home, as this would signal that books are purely decorative—and no one would want anyone to think that.

While books are central to the soul of a French home, art is integral to the soul of France. Indeed, Paris's renowned museums and highly respected art galleries have long been the art aficionado's paradise, and today the country is also a center for the global contemporary art scene. In the city of Tours in the Loire Valley, for example, the marketing tag line of a tourist board reads, "Time for Contemporary Art," courting new devotees. Moreover, there is tangible proof that the French have taken this message to heart. The terms *modern* and *contemporary* art are often used interchangeably but should not be. Modern art refers to works produced from the 1880s to the 1960s; the birth of contemporary art followed. Abstract art and expressionism created in the past fifty-some years suggest a sentiment, story, or memory.

As if moving with the times, oils, watercolors, and drawings—some more modest than others—passed down from one generation to the next, remain in place. Beyond that, however, awe-inspiring contemporary art serves as a further testament to the French passion for living artfully today.

OPPOSITE: Stunning in its simplicity, an entry with black-and-white marble inlay doubles as an art gallery. Cascading from above is a statement-making necklace of oversized, handblown Murano beads by lauded French artist Jean-Michel Othoniel, who recently created fountains for Versailles and whose works have been commissioned by Chanel, Louis Vuitton and Cartier. Nearby is a brass triangulation chair designed by internationally acclaimed Zhang Zhoujie, a pioneer in the realm of digital creativity.

ABOVE LEFT: A vessel of hyacinths complements hues in the oil by Margaret Evangeline. Arrangement is by Brenda Lyle.

ABOVE RIGHT: Distinctive objets d'art found at Jean de Merry add interest. Emitting light are Alexander Lamont's deeply faceted coupé vessels hewn from rock crystal blocks rich with inclusions. Gilding brings water-like clarity to the quartz.

RIGHT: An open-back settee covered in fabric by Pierre Frey and sofas bedecked in a Nancy Corzine silk look up to Murano glass leaf pendants from Galerie Glustin, Paris, that are suspended from the coffered ceiling. A 1970s table at Paris's sprawling Marché aux Puces de Saint-Ouen inspired the acrylic coffee table. Area rug is from Stark Carpet.

A signed and numbered Cy Twombly mixed-media lithograph hangs over the fireplace. Oil on canvas, 72 by 72 inches, with integrated, shimmering crystalline is the work of New York–based Margaret Evangeline.

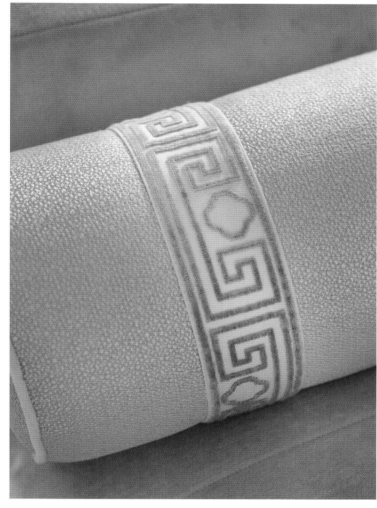

OPPOSITE: Approachable elegance, tranquil but edgy, reigns in a home with worldly sensibilities where antiques and contemporary art play a major role. Midcentury Russian armchairs wear their original fabric. French 40s coffee table is from Jan Showers. Custom-colored Fromental wallpaper—with ombré tints graduating from light to dark—serves as the backdrop for the work of Swiss artist Claudia Comte, whose eight elongated acrylics on canvas wrap the curved wall.

LEFT: Carving, gilding, and glazing collaborate to draw the eye.

RIGHT: A subtle detail softens the tailoring while dressing up the room. Lee Jofa tape circles a bolster covered in fabric by Pierre Frey.

ABOVE TOP: In high style, top-tacked window treatment boasts fabric from the French house of Manuel Canovas embellished with Samuel & Sons metallic tape. For an extra dash of glamour, shimmering wire-like fabric from Italy wraps custom acrylic rods and Louis XVI–inspired finials.

ABOVE BOTTOM: Embodying the spirit of modernity is a glimmering collection that merits a spot on the mantel. Exotic pink pyrite, unearthed in Peru, is extremely rare; pyrite with crystal quartz can also be difficult to come by. All stones are from Empressive GeoDesigns, Dallas.

RIGHT: A Murano chandelier from Galerie Glustin, Paris, hovers over a modern ebonized table that comfortably seats twelve. Dining chairs wear Montreal-based Theo Décor's lush velvet, defining what it means to be fashionable without being overly bold. Silk area rug from Stark Carpet is sufficiently large that chairs remain on the rug when guests leave the table. Cabinet by Allan Knight & Associates has a custom mocha lacquer finish with an overlay of silver ochre that ups the glamour.

ABOVE: *Concave Blue Mirror Disc*, by Frenchman Christophe Gaignon watches over a rare Austrian black-lacquered period commode, circa 1820, from Legacy Antiques. Also bedecking the hall is a 19th-century fauteuil in the style of Louis XVI, robed in fabric from Porter Teleo, Kansas City, which softens the gilding.

OPPOSITE: Artistic merit and style meet in a formal powder room, where dramatic hand-painted Gracie wallpaper dresses the walls. Not only does the large-scale pattern emit a contemporary spirit but it also creates the feeling of depth.

PREVIOUS OVERLEAF: As if proving that warmth trumps sleek minimalism, reclaimed oak beams lend a relaxed feeling to a casual living area that merges with the kitchen and breakfast room and opens to the pool, for easy indoor-outdoor living. Redefining a traditional ottoman is a practical glass tray that glides where needed.

ABOVE: Light plays off colors, furnishings, and textures differently. Some surfaces reflect light and some absorb it. Whether rough or smooth, brushed or burnished, each finish catches and reflects light in its own subtle way. A balance between shadow and light is essential in creating a becoming setting.

OPPOSITE: A mix of textures adds flair to a kitchen where a rooster takes center stage. Although mystery surrounds the reason he became an unofficial national symbol, most agree the French rooster represents both faith and light. The range hood is custom.

OPPOSITE: Working together, Colefax & Fowler, Romo and Taffard fabrics send an invitation to linger at a banquette that serves as a space saver in a high-traffic area. Custom Montesano armchairs surround an oval, limed oak table. Murano glass flower pendant by Cenedese is from Jean-Marc Fray.

ABOVE: Subtle tones unite the past—a glazed Swedish chest, circa 1830—and the present—contemporary art, an acrylic on canvas by Swiss-born Philippe Decrauzat. Urns from Mary Cates & Company, Dallas, deliver pattern to this side of the breakfast room. Without accessories, a room looks cold.

ABOVE: In His magnificently paneled library, rich mahogany lines the walls and moldings, much like in a gentlemen's club. Black lacquered settees are French, from Legacy Antiques, Dallas. They wear Jab Anstoetz fabric and Fadini Borghi welt. Desk is in the style of Louis XVI. Hide area rug is by Kyle Bunting, Austin.

OPPOSITE: Melding classic French architecture with innovative modernity, walls of glass offer a view into the wine room. Adding further luster to His library: brass pole lamps by Charles Hollis Jones from Cain Modern, West Hollywood, and Jim Thompson metallic window treatment with the sculptural look of crushed eggshells. Tailored trim is from Robert Allen.

OPPOSITE: Modern luxury is overnighting in a plush guest room where flowers abound. Schumacher wallcovering wraps the walls, while the headboard is intentionally solid. Blown glass bedside lamps are from Arteriors. Lusted-after blue Harlequin hydrangeas have a short growing season.

ABOVE: Whether from Holland, England, Prussia or China, distinctive blue-and-white porcelain is a coveted accessory.

BELOW LEFT: Striking Andrea Rosenberg art, Matouk bedding, and Arteriors blown-glass lamps spell luxury.

BELOW RIGHT: A cutout in the laundry room blends ingenuity with practicality—and in doing so outshines ordinary feline homes.

OPPOSITE: Contemporary Mondrian-like patterned millwork on bookcases divides the sleeping and lounge areas while complementing traditional egg-and-dart molding in the former. Chaises are from David Sutherland. The pole lamps are Ethan Allen. Warming both areas are amethyst sphere chandeliers with nickel accents by Ray Lockridge.

ABOVE: Jean-Marc Fray's antique Louis XVI mirrored chests and gray Murano lamps bring more than a bit of glamour into a spacious master bedroom with exquisite Gracie wallpaper. Oval, tight-back sofa with exposed, stained legs wears Fadini Borghi fabric.

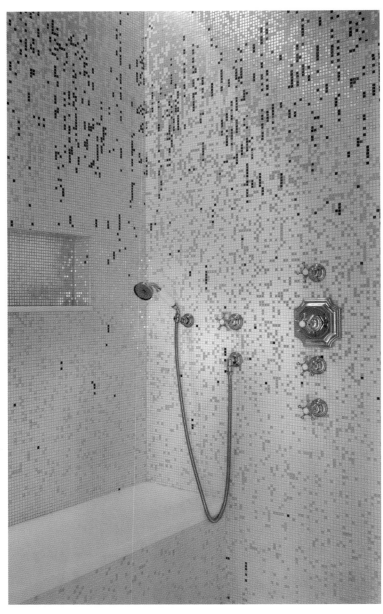

LEFT: A built-in dressing table boasts a Thassos countertop and customized drawers that house outlets for a hair dryer and more.

RIGHT: A spacious shower flaunts eye-catching tile produced by Artaic Tile. The Boston-based company is known for bringing the ancient art of mosaic into the modern age. Showerheads (unseen) on the opposite wall allow the homeowners to set the preferred water temperature without getting wet.

OPPOSITE: Mahogany frames His bath, where an undercounter basin from the Mick de Giulio Collection for Kallista has the look of gently flowing water. Low-profile faucet is from Waterworks.

LEFT: A custom swing bed paired with fabric from John Robshaw Textiles emit a spirit equal to other rooms of the house. Pendant is by Made Goods and area rug is from Decorative Carpets.

ABOVE: Dazzling, swirling beading and sequins adorn a linen pouf from Global Views. Following the family's recent trip to Africa, a giraffe joined the intimate conversation spot.

ABOVE: A self-serve snack/coffee/juice/margarita bar raises outdoor entertaining to a new level.

RIGHT: Inspired by the French architecture of the main house, a (dog-friendly) family area creates the ultimate outdoor space.

OPPOSITE: Decked in all-weather fabrics, stylish Janus et Cie table and chairs lift alfresco dining to sophisticated new heights. Sun-drenched swing is from Dedon. The pool house setting lends itself to the relaxed look of banana leaves and ginger, an arrangement by Brenda Lyle.

LEFT: Statement-making coral mirror from Made Goods and sea glass basket-weave wall tile from Antique Floors lend luster and panache to a pool bath by introducing a multitude of textures. Stacked banana-fiber cushions from Ikea work for sitting poolside.

RIGHT: Stone walls ensure privacy in an outdoor shower accessible through the pool house. Translucent sea glass tile—irregular in shape—is from Ann Sacks.

CHIC, FRESH, AND INVITING

*I*t is easy to fall under the influence of the French, who bring inherent style to most everything they do. Reflecting a rich cultural heritage, their celebrated approach to living, dressing, and dining well is as distinctive as their decorating, which is undeniably chic.

Seemingly, French chic is everywhere lately. Exquisitely fashioned, hand-forged iron railings, unassuming stone fireplaces, reclaimed wood floors, and sculpted fittings perched on hotel-inspired washstands are among the many noble accents captivating those of us living on this side of the Atlantic.

Pointedly taking cues from the French, Stateside artisans replicate old-world textures on walls and reproduce coveted paint effects like glazing, which reflects light differently from paint depending upon the base and top coats used. These days, however, glazed walls most often serve as backdrops for furnishings from disparate eras that work together in an inviting way rather than as milieus for painstakingly carved armoires, generously scaled commodes, and sophisticated Louis chairs. In a noted shift, midcentury and modern-day pieces worthy of standing ovations are not only elevating looks but also playing starring roles.

As some still struggle to get it right, we have learned that balance, or the equal distribution of weight, is key to fashioning a serene, welcoming room. Unless furnishings find their way to the right places, their considerable presence can be unwelcoming, slanting the visual weight to one side of a room. Either scale (size) or proportion (shape) can result in a setting that looks "off"—or in other words, with an image problem that is hard to pinpoint.

Furniture, fabrics, floor coverings, and accessories of artistic merit vie with one another for the pleasure of introducing color to settings. Nevertheless, it is most often compelling *fabric*—reportedly stemming from the French *fabriqué,* "the created world"—that sets the mood. In homes where the old and new join forces to create a certain mystique, splashy patterns are commonly eschewed in favor of monochromatic simplicity, as light, subtle patterns appear more serene than do those with obvious contrast. What's more, a discreet mix fosters interest, while fabrics that meld rather than match give depth to a room without overwhelming the space.

As indulgences go, we embrace sumptuous silks, relaxed linens, and unpretentious cottons expertly woven in the textile epicenter of Lyon, France, if not in mills near Como, Italy, or the US. Pairing dressy fabrics with textured, more casual ones texts the message that an approachable, livable feeling is central to our designs.

In the Île-de-France—the historic heart and most populous hub of the country—smoldering grays, creams, and muted, low-saturated earth tones typically anchor settings. Far-from-intense values of this color family appeals to the sensibilities of Parisians, whose cosmopolitan style requires that wall finishes, fabrics, and furnishings simply complement each other rather than compete for attention.

For a romantic air, the look may refreshingly include a pastel. Rather than pair a muted shade with other pastels, most prefer mixing one with airy whites, ivories, parchment, and all manner of pale grays and putties, which can also prove a soothing foil to stronger, more distinctive colors.

Bright, colorful accents are at home on the French Riviera in the beach cities of Nice and Cannes, where many longtime residents use a punch of color to shore up sites flooded with light—tempered with quieter tints.

Contrary to common belief, those living in Provence also shy away from intense, saturated hues—although outsiders continue to associate Provence with the brilliantly colored Provençal

PREVIOUS OVERLEAF: Distinctly Parisian, a curated mix of the relaxed and refined, the past and present includes a place for guests to place their handbags. The glazed, late-19th-century bench sits beneath an oversized antique mirror, reflecting a Murano pendant, circa 1970. Oil painting by Susie Pryor, Atlanta, pulls color from the garden beyond. Stone flooring and baseboard varies in tone from cool cream to dove gray to warm honey. Blonde Barr, a natural limestone, sailed from France to Paris Ceramics, NYC, before winding its way into this entry.

OPPOSITE: An 18th-century *cheminée* from a *maison* in the Loire Valley—imported by Pittet Architecturals, Dallas—anchors a room that exudes a fresh, uncluttered aesthetic. Firebrick set in a herringbone pattern lines the firebox, stacked with birch logs. Coffee table is from Formations, table lamp from Donghia, pole lamp from Baker Furniture. The setting served as inspiration for accents of green, including the elongated pillow from Pierre Frey. Swivel chairs offer the option of joining one of two conversation groups, while a throw from Schweitzer Linen adds both an accent color and warmth.

florals and paisleys that have draped outdoor markets in a charming way ever since Avignon became home to Souleiado textiles. It is not that these prints are off-limits; only that for a while now, habitués have been gravitating to palettes both muted and restrained. In vogue are earthy tones of sand, clay, biscuit, fawn, café au lait, and mushroom, which appear bleached by the sun in the region's strong light.

As it happens, texture has a reputation for shaping rooms much like color. Almost certainly, a room with few textures produces the feeling of space; however, a setting with all sleek finishes is standoffish and unavoidably cold. Integrating disparate materials can be a challenge, mostly because layering furniture, fabrics, and lighting requires pulling together myriad variations of rough and smooth, to say nothing of light and dark, hard and soft, matte and shiny, and refined and relaxed. Unless there is an adroit mix of both contrasting and complementary surfaces, a setting can be disconcerting or even jarring, or perhaps worse, horribly flat.

PREVIOUS OVERLEAF: Dissimilar seating groups and a mix of furnishings from various eras emit a less-than-formal look in an airy space ideal for relaxing. A Louis XIV limestone *cheminée* mingles with present-day custom steel doors, framed in Zoffany fabric that flows from an iron rod by Iron Age, Dallas. Laying the foundation for élan: a Holland & Sherry flat-woven hemp area rug that unifies the seating groups.

OPPOSITE: The humble lamp shade looks noticeably smarter constructed in fabric, with a contrasting trim further amping up its look. Adding a complementary lining can also set a shade apart; however, the density of the fabric will influence the amount of light emanating from the lamp. All lamps in a room should finish at approximately the same height, varying not more than an inch or two.

ABOVE: No longer do Americans transport armoires across the ocean with offers of refashioned images conforming to stateside tastes. Instead, we host flat screen televisions and other electronics in full view. Hand-finished plaster walls serve as background for noticeably sophisticated but unassuming furnishings. Print on chairs is by Romo. Coveted fringed cashmere throw is from D. Porthault. Pole lamp is from Baker Furniture.

ABOVE: Attached to the past, the French treasure hand-me-downs from family that offer the reassuring feeling of the familiar. However, they also prize disparate accessories and art picked up in their travels. Small but captivating Murano vase is from Jan Showers. Arrangement is by Fiddlehead Designs in Cashiers, NC, a local go-to.

OPPOSITE: Whether it's the deft use of books or other attention-grabbing accoutrements, accessories help make a room more interesting. Here, an elongated onyx bowl propped with sand, rocks, and succulents is a modest addition to the coffee table and the nature-inspired palette.

It is fitting, then, that in expressing a taste for fresh modernity, artistry demands juxtaposing soft, sensuous surfaces among those perceived severe—the more subtly, the better—to add energy to the room. Since rough textures are most apt to warm a setting, an area rug with less-than-smooth fibers topped by a coffee table with a luxe reflective surface might be a start. At the same time, a tall, mellow wood piece can ground a room awash in light walls.

In keeping with our contemporary lifestyles, we ardently sculpt satisfying rooms that dismiss a singular style or period. Pairing the glamorous and the less-than-perfect together with a mix of paintings, drawings, and photographs fashions a look that is a work of art on its own. Another secret? Striking details that add polish to everything from table settings to bed linens, from upholstery to window treatments and floor coverings.

Certainly, our true achievement is each room's individuality that sends a message about who we are. For this, we thank our design allies the French, for their ever-so-chic way of expressing both beauty and taste from which we have learned.

ABOVE: With French-style attention to detail, rows of Great Plains tape—the narrower set above the wider—add a level of interest to loveseats covered in a Rogers & Goffigon linen.

OPPOSITE: In keeping with modern living, a vintage bar cart from Bergdorf Goodman stands in for a table in a spot where the latter would have been a tight squeeze. The Baccarat votive topping cocktail recipe books is by the French design megastar Philippe Starck, famous for his take on a Louis XVI fauteuil known as the Louis Ghost.

Sunlight spills across the Paris Ceramics stone flooring and base, and onto *gris clair* (soft gray) textured walls—the backdrop for artwork by Susie Pryor, central to the dining area's design. Baccarat pendants worthy of name-dropping top *très chic* marble tables supported by iron bases—fitting a Parisian café. C&C Milano print and Zoffany apple green solid cover klismos chairs. Thanks to Marroquin Upholstery, Dallas, the statement-making, curved-back, Greek-inspired chairs with splayed back legs are perfectly scaled to the tables.

OPPOSITE: At Les Deux Magots and Café de Flore—famed Left Bank tourist destinations once favored as rendezvous spots of the literary and intellectual elite—round tables 40 inches in diameter encourage intimate conversations from early morning until well after midnight. Low-absorption Ruivina marble tabletop works for both exterior and interior applications.

ABOVE: Open-weave "Labyrinth Crystal" from London-based Chase Erwin flanks steel doors, diffusing light and soliciting admiring glances. Curtains that puddle or pool no longer work in contemporary settings. (The difference between curtains and draperies? Although both are window coverings, curtains are lighter, thinner or sheerer. Since curtains aren't lined, they don't block the light, nor do they guarantee privacy. Drapes exude a more formal look.)

PREVIOUS OVERLEAF: White or unobtrusive gray is often the go-to color of Parisian kitchens. Given a compact nature, most are void of bold color, which means there's no chance of their appearing dated. As a new generation of high-performance appliances—ranges, microwaves, warming drawers, dishwashers, refrigerators, freezers and wine coolers—transform stateside kitchens, the popularity of open-plan living continues to grow.

LEFT: Befitting the setting, staggered 4 x 16-inch honed Calacatta Gold tiles with pronounced gray veining run up walls, while fabricated slab casing frames steel windows. Mesh vegetable basket is from Waterworks. Herbs in the mirrored glass containers rest on marble sills.

RIGHT: Honed three-centimeter Calacatta Gold marble slabs—treated with Dupont stain protection—hold glass canisters from The Container Store. Artfully rolled Williams-Sonoma linens are an everyday luxury ready to be called into use. Hardware is by Schaub.

OPPOSITE: While we find it difficult to curb an appetite for gleaming stainless steel commercial ranges, Parisians tend to embrace energy-efficient, cold-to-the-touch induction cooktops—deemed safer when small children are in the home. Oversized culinary utensils are staples in French kitchens, often from E. Dehillerin.

OPPOSITE: Escaping the formality of a traditional dining area, a sports bar topped with stainless steel is suited for reading the newspaper, offering snacks and serving family-style meals. Stemware from Ralph Lauren Home and Baccarat park on lead-free Starphire shelves, while mirrors double the look. Pendants are Baccarat. Adding interest are three-dimensional papier-mâché sculptures by French artist Philippe Balayn: *Crabe Royal du Kamtchatka* and *Caviar Imperial Beluga.*

ABOVE: Glazing lends an old-world aura to textured, hand-plastered walls, while an intriguing, German-made Qlocktwo wall clock upstages most other clocks by unexpectedly revealing the time in words. Herb watercolors are by Israeli artist Yael Berger. Baccarat pendants (two unseen) hang over the island housing a sink, two dishwashers, recycling bin, and storage.

ABOVE: Stacks of humble, waffle-weave guest towels from Pottery Barn readily handle a crowd.

BELOW: Hand-embroidered D. Porthault linen guest towels convert an everyday powder room into a more sophisticated epicenter.

OPPOSITE: Waterworks wall mount fittings and Lawson sink look up to a grouping of playfully configured glass pendants from ABC Carpet, NYC. Together, the custom teak washstand and teak mirror splash the space with warmth, while textured Phillip Jeffries wallcovering imparts an upbeat air.

OPPOSITE: Steps from a door leading into the garage, a mudroom bench offers a spot to put on running or golf shoes, while hand-painted pillow fabric by Gillian Bradshaw Smith makes an artistic statement. The importance Bentley, a Norwich Terrier, plays in this family is hard to miss.

ABOVE: Waterdrop wallcovering by Pollack puts its own spin on washday with tile from the Renaissance Collection and pedestals from Miele—for easier loading and convenient storage—elevating the look of a compact laundry. In Europe, the washer and dryer often reside under a kitchen countertop.

BELOW: Some say that nowhere is the impulse to spoil one's most loyal friend more apparent than in France. However, countless stateside dogs lead equally privileged lives. To be sure, MacKenzie-Child's upscale "Courtly Check" enamelware can make a pet feel special. Though many Parisians consider it gauche to take home leftovers, in a sign of the times, the French government recently passed a bill requiring bistros and cafés to offer patrons "le doggie bag."

Black and white—familiar yet fresh—create an impact with help from Stark Carpet, which lays the groundwork for a workspace exuding femininity. With its sophisticated silhouette, a floating Paris desk pays homage to the French 1940s. Fashion-forward pink velvet from the venerable house of Pierre Frey warms the chair. Ralph Lauren easel flanks the sofa, plumped with pillows. Layered lighting (desk lamp by Koncept, table lamp from Chameleon wearing Fortuny shade, and London-made Hector Finch chandelier) amps up the luminescence of Maya Romanoff wallpaper. Ideal for holding magazines is a vintage accessory from Jan Showers.

An important aside: before hanging any fixture—antique or not—check the wiring and make sure it is UL approved. Underwriters Laboratories is the trusted source for product compliance.

LEFT: Artfully framed, fashion-savvy watercolors by Cape Town, South African artist Gabrielle Raaff, nod to the style of the French.

RIGHT: Rows of Samuel & Sons perfectly scaled pearl trim add a dash of glamour to the Création Baumann window treatment, while contrasting welt lends a bit of theater to the Rogers & Goffigon sofa fabric.

OPPOSITE: The stainless steel étagère and Paris desk—both projecting a French Forties air— make up Her personal space. Gucci picture frames, circa 1950, from Jan Showers and leather frames from Helene Batoff, Wynnewood, PA, create a mini photo gallery. William Yeoward vase with fresh blooms adds to the beauty of the room.

OPPOSITE: Applying Sherle Wagner wallpaper horizontally in the main area and vertically in the adjoining water closet gives this guest powder an unconventional, au courant spin that makes the space appear larger. Honed Calacatta Veechi washstand hosts a Waterworks basin set and polished nickel sink. Covetable vintage sconces from Chameleon Lighting further enhance the mood, as light from diverse levels creates ambiance.

ABOVE LEFT: Hand-embroidered linen guest towels from D. Porthault pay homage to an abundance of frogs that roam in the nearby lake.

ABOVE RIGHT: Moderne crystal "icicle" pendant is from Chameleon.

LEFT: Dazzling, attention-grabbing, red-striped Murano pendant illuminates its surroundings while setting the tone for the powder room's design. The Mazzega fixture, circa 1960, was found at the Paris Flea Market.

ABOVE: Layering Roman shades and curtains spells luxury. An opaque lining known as blackout and hidden interlining unite to help prevent sun damage to the Jim Thompson stripe. Expertly applied Houlès trims add interest, give bedroom windows presence, and pay homage to the influence of the French.

RIGHT: A master both elegant and edgy exudes contemporary flair, prompted by Jim Thompson's dramatic horizontal stripe and Stark Carpet sisal laid on the diagonal. Veritas glass lamps wear custom shades by Cele Johnson, Dallas. Glazing gave once-nondescript chests with inset antique mirrors a more modern identity while offering assurance that there would be no worries about drinks staining the chests. Mounting the window treatment as close to the ceiling as possible creates the illusion of height, as does painting moldings the same color as the walls.

Diamond tufting underscores the appeal of an upholstered headboard whose height is a modern update on classic style. Tufting is the age-old process of drawing a cord through fabric to create a cushioned look with highs and lows. Here, buttons and piping add interest.

ABOVE: Where better to mindfully refresh than in the ultimate getaway—a chaise? Nesting tables offer the perfect spot to prop a drink while a floor lamp from Ralph Lauren Home is positioned just so for reading. Completing the layered look is a contrasting throw. Furnishings, however attractive, look best when varied in height, whether the setting is a living area or bedroom, classic or contemporary.

OPPOSITE: *Meditation*, a grouping of sixteen oils by Michelle Gagliano of Scottsville, VA, and Nobilis wallcovering bring dimension to the master bedroom. Tiered pendant with a strong silhouette is vintage. Bentley, a Norwich Terrier, favors Perennial floor pillows for napping.

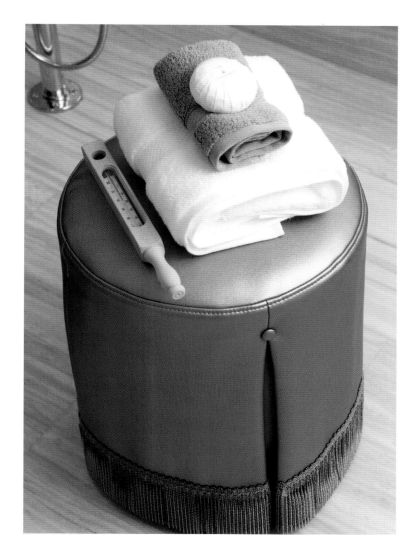

OPPOSITE: Her bath basks in natural light while overflowing with calming details. Waterworks cast-iron bateau soaking tub reads France, while the Murano pendant reads Italy. Oregon-based Hartmann & Forbes wallcovering floats above stone stacked walls, as radiant heat warms stone flooring that accommodates a shapely Bloomingdale's hamper. Dressing up the room's aesthetic appeal is an oversized, full-length mirror.

LEFT: A humble bath stool morphs into one more glamorous with the addition of eye-catching Kravet metallic trim. After making its debut more than 5,000 years ago in Mesopotamia, fringe has appeared in fashionable interiors for centuries now. Perfect for testing the water: a bath thermometer from Waterworks.

RIGHT: A Waterworks polished nickel floor-mounted tub filler emits old-world poise.

OPPOSITE: With a playfulness that is engaging—and ample light courtesy of the oversized steel window—an intimate space works for playing bridge, Chinese checkers, or board games. Edgy resin-and-acrylic contemporary art is by Sandra Looney; oiled walnut game table with matte finish is from Richard Wrightman, NYC. Credit Marroquin Upholstery, Dallas, with precisely centering the painterly Christian Fischbacher patterned fabric on each custom-painted chair and outlining its shape with Samuel & Sons gimp. Signed Venini pendant, circa 1971, is from John Gregory.

ABOVE: Photographs send a message about the importance of family. On a wall with narrow shelving, light flows through seamless acrylic Prisma frames—both contemporary and dated—highlighting the family's recent trip to Botswana and far-from-wild get-togethers elsewhere.

PREVIOUS OVERLEAF: Hartmann Forbes cork wraps den walls, while handsomely woven Ralph Lauren water hyacinth sectional pays homage to fashionable French Forties designs. Also from Ralph Lauren, leather table lamps resting on teak side tables. Perennials tape adds texture and depth to linen window treatment by Straight Stitch, Dallas. Anchoring the room is an area rug from Eliko Rugs, NYC, with a soft spot for the family's Norwich terrier. Further elevating the mood: gallery-wrapped oil on canvas of a zebra by Canadian artist Andre Petterson.

LEFT: Metal-studded Phillip Jeffries wallpaper envelopes His office bath, with Adnet leather mirror from Blanchetti, Paris, supplying even more texture. The strike-off— or test sample produced to offer a preview of the color and scale when woven—from Eliko Rugs serves as the mat seen here.

RIGHT: Walnut and brass pulls from Waterworks have a masculine air.

OPPOSITE: For Him, a handsome Richard Wrightman desk with clean lines and a canvas blotter. Midcentury modern Eames desk chair from Design Within Reach was reupholstered in brown leather. Hinting of the look inside the room is a photo of giraffes.

Fine Paints of Europe's Hollandlac Brilliant 1798, a rich navy lacquer with mirror-like luminescence, envelopes walls, teaming with white to make a striking statement. Graphic-patterned area rug is from Stark Carpet. Window treatment, blanket cover, and shams wear C&C Milano; bed hangings are from Etamine, with linens by Ralph Lauren. Layered textures create the French signature look, while contrast of light and dark adds drama to a room with midcentury modern steel bed, desk, and luggage racks.

OPPOSITE: Glossy navy lacquered walls lend a glamorous air to a peaceful spot overlooking a lake. Donghia slipper chair and ottoman wear Bergamo fabric. Throw is from D. Porthault. Window treatment stacks to the right, permitting a cigar aficionado access to the deck.

ABOVE: *Sunday Morning*—a grouping of three oils on canvas by Austin artist Hallie Eubanks—ups the degree of modernity with support from the woven chair from Janus et Cie.

ABOVE: Geometric-patterned Quadrille wallpaper teams with Matouk towels, energizing a guest bath with twin polished nickel basins by Waterworks.

OPPOSITE: Earthy neutrals partner with Phillip Jeffries Zebra Grass wallpaper, bringing texture and depth to a Balinese-inspired room that offers the comfort of a luxury hotel. Breezy Rogers & Goffigon Trade Winds linen, fabricated into bed hanging, adds a bit of romance to the masterfully crafted bed. Lined and interlined curtains ensure that guests do not wake up with the birds.

OPPOSITE: Fashionable and fun Tolomeo Mega arc lamp elevates the look while leaving plenty of desk space. Luggage stand is from Pottery Barn, recovered in GH Leather. Formations vessel hosts a mix of untamed flowers.

LEFT: Contemporary lines and stylish furnishings meld with fabrics, wallpaper, succulents, and woven accessories from travels to exude an artistic spirit.

RIGHT: Layered textures—rough and smooth, hard and soft, tight and loosely woven—complement the beauty and easy-going ways of Bali. Leather-wrapped vessels are from Urban Zen.

ABOVE: Working together, natural light, plush towels, and a ladder from Roost deliver character to a bath. Layering related stone and base with textured wall covering further enhances the space. The water closet is in its own dedicated room.

RIGHT: A bateau tub, separate shower, plump Sferra towels, and acrylic abstracts by Atlanta artist Britt Bass conspire to help a guest relax. Applying the same stone in the shower as in the main area visually magnifies the space.

PREVIOUS OVERLEAF: Classic and modern finishes join forces, connecting with nature from the ground up to create a tranquil atmosphere. Phillip Jeffries warm burlap clads the walls. Skilled weavers sculpted the oversize chandelier for Made Goods. Handsome Formations bed boasts

restful tones and a blend of textures that bring laid-back tranquility to the space. On the headboard: rich brown GH Leather. Tray table is by Richard Wrightman. Laying the cowhide rug on a diagonal gives the room a contemporary bent.

OPPOSITE: Pierre Frey fabric has unrivaled charm. Cowhide area rug from Designer Carpets, Atlanta, delivers an extra layer of texture. Drink table is from Gregorius Pineo.

ABOVE: Stone pulls paired with a weathered washboard from Botswana blend with the palette and produce rustic appeal.

Widely lauded Perennials fabric (on sofa) and whimsical Quadrille (on chairs) are both weather friendly and family friendly. Also crafted to withstand the elements while not forgoing style: the Elliot Bay table lamps (one unseen) and Serena & Lily polypropylene, mildew-resistant area rug, defining the space that opens to the lake.

Menu

Soup
Chilled gazpacho garnished
with tarragon

Salad
kale beet salad with citrus, pistachio,
goat cheese and fresh mint

Main
fresh salmon with julienne carrots,
couscous and a
lemon dill caper cream

Dessert
crème brulee sprinkled with
homegrown strawberries and
grand marnier

ABOVE: Menu cards make an intimate gathering even more memorable, and they are easy to make with today's technology.

OPPOSITE: When the weather turns warm, it's time to move an informal gathering to an informal spot. Reclaimed wood beams add warmth and architectural interest, elevating a screened porch from everyday to extraordinary. For optimal airflow, the Casablanca ceiling fans are set 9 feet from the ground. Television is weatherproof.

OPPOSITE: No matter that France has long touted its bottled waters—Evian and Perrier. Aiming to reduce plastic waste as well as aid digestion, the French have been installing a sparkling water fountain, or *fontaine pétillante,* in each of Paris's twenty arrondissements. Crowd-pleasing bar cart stocked with entertaining essentials rests on Thar stone—indigenous to India. Oils on wood of birds native to North Carolina are by Kathleen Buys, Houston.

ABOVE LEFT: A farmers market luncheon has more than a side of style. For those with a passion for modern design, Pottery Barn's square dinnerware layers perfectly. No matter whether produce is from one's own garden or a local market, gathering friends to catch up is important.

ABOVE RIGHT: A luncheon isn't complete without dessert, and no trip to France is complete without a visit to a *boulangerie* or *pâtisserie*. Fortunately, both are omnipresent or abundant in France. Here, crème brûlée—a custard base topped with hardened caramel—adorns a Buccellati tray.

LEFT: Party-ready Wolf grill stands ready to please the family or a crowd. Soapstone slabs decking the countertop host Old Bay Seasoning sculpture by Karen Shapiro, represented by various US galleries.

MODERN-DAY MAGNETISM

After long upholding tradition, or seldom straying from the well-practiced belief that the past must be present, hosting the new is the ever-widening French mantra. As the twenty-first century continues to unfold, sumptuously accessorized rooms filled with weighty furniture and voluminous draperies (embellished with swags and jabots) often feel static, stuffy, and, rather bluntly, overdone. Halting the monotony of old-world décor are streamlined silhouettes, strategic use of color, and works of art that emit a relaxed yet refined au courant aesthetic.

Literally breathing fresh air into centuries-old Parisian *appartements* that brim with architectural reminders of the space's former life are marble, glass, stone, and metal surfaces in a range of finishes including bronze and burnished brass. Natural materials such as clay, leather, and bleached wood also lend dimension and deliver warmth to dwellings, where appreciation for handmade tiles, handwoven baskets, and coveted linens spotlight the captivating way the French live today.

Electrifying modern and contemporary canvases help make settings in gentrified areas one's own—as bursts of saturated shades work well against the preferred backdrop of neutral walls. Since one doesn't often see strong color on walls, it stands to follow that a graphic canvas with bold strokes and riotous color can transform even the most staid space into a room that reverberates with life.

PREVIOUS OVERLEAF: White linen curtains frame entry doors that open to the street, while white plaster walls flow freely from room to room, melding the home's interiors with the homeowners' art changing the palette. The artwork of internationally acclaimed Peter Keil makes a strong visual statement in addition to serving as a conversation starter. A Créations Métaphores velvet ombré—fabric with gradations light to dark— covers a bench produced by Matizza's Upholstery, Houston, that rests on newly quarried Belgium blue limestone laid in a rhythmic pattern.

RIGHT: Streamlined steel doors heighten the view while adding a midcentury edge to open-plan living, with distinct areas for gathering and dining. Plump, velvet pillows rest on a sofa with classic lines, while chaise and chairs project a modern look. All textiles are dog-friendly Perennials Fabrics, including the eggplant pillows. The statement piece—a mirrored coffee table—hosts well-read books.

Once Aubusson (flat-woven) carpets and Savonnerie (knotted-pile) area rugs, as well as a range of Persian-style rugs with intricate geometric motifs, delivered color to French interiors. A more modern take on floorcoverings includes monochromatic or ombré styles in anything from silk to fluffy flokati (a woolen rug with thick, loose pile, woven in Greece).

When it comes to texture, some surfaces reflect light and some absorb it. Whether rough or smooth, brushed or burnished, each finish catches and reflects light in its own way, however subtle. A balance between shadow and light is essential in creating a becoming setting.

In a similar fashion, textiles in today's French homes increasingly rely on texture, sheen, or hue rather than pattern or motif. Much like a pristine white wall, a clean-lined sofa upholstered in a quality, solid-color fabric is stylistically chic.

OPPOSITE: In this era of merging sensibilities, old meets new when reclaimed wood tops a table supported by an acrylic base. The custom dining table is from Vieux Interiors, Houston. Chairs from Ikea rest on the pleasingly bare floor. Inset steel firewood door and threshold—integrated in the flooring—create the illusion that the fireplace is wood burning. Pendant is Murano.

ABOVE: For a fresh, up-to-the-minute look, pots of ornamental oregano from the local garden center fill a square glass container lined with burlap.

ABOVE: Hand-painting on the reverse side of glass—known as *églomisé*, with reflective properties (in this case gold, silver, and copper leaf) and origins dating back to medieval times—by Timothy Poe, Birmingham, AL, resides above a high-backed banquette upholstered in Harlequin fabric. Faux-fur pillows enhance the comfort, with sculpted accent tables delivering a contemporary twist.

RIGHT: Natural light floods a sumptuous living area with two distinct but harmonious seating groups. The versatile chaise functions as a room divider, while the Perennials area rug not only grounds the room but also promises no worries about spills or stains. Sliding barn doors (left) separate the dining and family living spaces from the kitchen.

OPPOSITE: Pasadena-based Lawson-Fenning midcentury chairs wear Edelman cognac leather. Pillows pick up the undertones of birch logs. A tidy row of Hermès throws—held in place with vintage French meat hooks—relaxes the look while standing ready for tastings when the antique door from Chateau Domingue, Houston, opens to the wine room. Flooring is reclaimed oak. Trending today: Integrated base flush with the plaster and settings without crown molding.

LEFT: Arteriors barstools and Visual Comfort brushed-brass pendants meet in an intimate bar, where aged-wood flooring and leathered-marble countertops join exposed brick walls in framing views of olive trees.

RIGHT: Bar powder room boasts classic black-and-white marble flooring that once lined a hotel in France, while quartzite vanity, bronze basin, and fittings from Hollywood Hardware exude modern flair. The Urban Electric pendant casts light on Benjamin Moore 1253 "Fresco Urbain" lacquered walls. The art? Stem of a wine glass dipped in red wine produced the results.

ABOVE: When company calls, accessing the finest wines is convenient, thanks to a ladder that smoothly glides along an iron bar. The tasting room's poured concrete walls with gray slurry overlay create the appearance of age.

OPPOSITE: A tasting room maintains old-world charm while adding a bit of contemporary flair to its welcoming tone. Houstonian Cindy Witmer designed the custom elongated table built by Vieux Interiors. Flooring is glazed concrete. Highly protective of its vineyards, French ordinances prohibit foreign buyers from purchasing winery-related properties without government approval.

LEFT: Honed-marble slabs cascade down sides of an island in waterfall fashion, adding more than a modicum of drama to an airy, light-filled kitchen. French-style open shelving supported by brass-plated posts offers easy access to everyday needs. Art simply leans against the walls. Brass and leather bar stools are from J. Alexander, Los Angeles; antique pendants from Back Row Home, Houston.

ABOVE: Hosting a dazzling array of sugars is a tiered, *très moderne*, French pastry stand.

ABOVE: Brass fittings and oversized pulls bring a bit of glam to an integrated sink with a built-in shelf ideal for hosting hand soap. For a clean, modern aesthetic, an eased-edge profile—slightly rounded, not sharp—is a popular option, as is honed versus polished marble. Honed marble lacks the reflective qualities of polished marble, yet it is less porous and not easily scratched.

OPPOSITE: Four doors (two unseen) that can be configured in multiple ways glide effortlessly, separating the open-plan kitchen from the gathering areas. The doors remain open unless the family is entertaining, in which case they are closed. An 18th-century stone *chiminée* that once resided in a *maison de maître* in Lille, France, now serves as a vent hood.

OPPOSITE: Most every room can benefit from a touch of the unexpected. Here, pull-out steps lead the way to a snug, not quite secret alcove, where a child could happily read a book while a parent cooks, or a pet could be content napping or simply watching. Duralee faux-leather trim garnishing Schumacher Belgian linen bed hangings gives the area distinct charm.

ABOVE LEFT: Behind closed Schumacher Belgian linen panels are cereal, crackers, and coffee—or a pantry that foregoes a traditional door or cabinets.

ABOVE RIGHT: In keeping with the French need for organization, serving pieces (on the opposite wall) remain dust-free and ready to be called into service at a moment's notice, thanks to a curtain.

LEFT: In a catering kitchen designed for entertaining, the refrigerator stands party-ready with beverages.

OPPOSITE: In a family-friendly media room apportioned into areas for watching movies and playing the centuries-old table game of backgammon, the sectional is covered in a Robert Allen cotton velvet. On the ceiling is Sherwin Williams "Red Cent" 6341, not exactly the burnt orange that is the official color of The University of Texas, but close.

ABOVE LEFT: Propped on an easel found on eBay, "Beautiful Day" poster wins rave reviews, as does the Samuel & Sons nailhead-studded tape masking seams of Joseph Noble faux leather. Data shows France—the most visited country on earth—has become a hotspot for film crews. In 2017, more than 5,000 photo shoots took place, mainly in Paris and the Provence-Alpes-Côte d'Azure region.

ABOVE RIGHT: Postal boxes that once welcomed mail to a small Texas town are now inset in a hall wall, where they garner interest while holding smartphones, chargers, keys, and more.

LEFT: Reclaimed oak floors, hand scraped with gray glaze, take a sharp turn toward the media room while adding character and warmth to the home.

LEFT: In Houston, an open-air pool house can be an enticing place to dine and entertain most anytime of the year. Here, low-maintenance Astroturf is an economical alternative to grass.

ABOVE: Nature's clear cypress with multiple knots takes center stage in a powder that works with both the pool and media room. Custom trough sink by Gunnells Concrete Designs, Houston, complements the laid-back luxury look.

ABOVE: Glazed wood on treads pairs well with slurried-brick risers, linking the first and second floors. Design of wrought-iron stair rail complements the steel windows and fresh look of the home.

RIGHT: Custom chests flank the master headboard upholstered in Jerry Pair leather. Eggplant felt from Kravet covers the master chaise, while a geometric area rug from Matt Camron Rugs & Tapestries warms the floor.

LEFT: Her fondness for both Hermès and horses inspired a closet with the look of a luxury boutique. Chaise sports Place Textiles and Houlès leather piping. The latter outlines both the cushion and Hermès fabric-wrapped bolster.

ABOVE LEFT: Clothing resides behind closed curtains, while a saddle purchased in France joins Hermès accessories in highlighting the homeowner's personal interests.

ABOVE RIGHT: Her office walls sport Lucite cases where a mother and daughter's shared love for horses is on display. Awe-inspiring ribbons and trophies rotate following competitive events.

ABOVE: The removable top of the French Art Deco bar cart, circa 1940, serves as a tray for entertaining, while the four swivel sides serve as wine glass storage.

RIGHT: In the master sitting area, elongated shelving on the left balances bookshelves and a stained door on the opposite side of the fireplace—in the same way two chairs on the right offset the sofa to the left. Siding with the asymmetrical shelving, a bronze coffee table from High Fashion Home, Houston, spells luxury.

OVERLEAF: A white-on-white spa-like aesthetic inspired a far from basic integrated tub—with a ledge for bath salt, soap, and greenery, and shelves for absorbent Egyptian cotton towels and art. His and Her built-in vanities store necessities.

LEFT: In a room belonging to a champion rider, chests from Pottery Barn flank a bed accessorized in lavender tones. When showing Hunter Jumpers, monogrammed collars (in frame propped on chest) are a necessary part of attire. The bench in the style of Louis XVI is vintage. Fittingly, bits forming the letter "H" on throw pillow pay homage to Hunter Jumpers and horses in general.

ABOVE: Slurried, exposed-brick walls meander into a teen's room with high ceilings and oversized lantern that adds warmth. Houstonian Bill Peck fabricated the lantern designed by architectural consultant Sarah West.

ABOVE LEFT: Built-in storage drawers for seasonal clothes readily maximize space.

ABOVE RIGHT: Custom barn door hardware is from Fixtures and Fittings, Houston.

BELOW LEFT: When an alert teen spotted two puppies in the middle of the highway, she pulled to the side of the road, gathered them in her arms and brought them home. In an effort to locate the owners, the family posted signs, advertised in the paper, and had a vet check for chips. All proved fruitless, but by then it was puppy love, so the girl's family kept one, and the other went to a relative living nearby. The tent for Luna and Zoe was a gift from grandparents.

OPPOSITE: A Lucite table—a modern take on the classic corner table—filled with championship ribbons prompts awe and admiration. A patterned runner grounds the intimate seating area.

GLOBAL PRESENCE

The French may forever favor furnishings crafted within *l'Hexagone,* but the cultural fusion in their homes reflects their artistic spirit, discerning eye, and worldly tastes. With an ardor for travel, they have a gift for imbuing settings with a meaningful mix of global finds exuding exotic or bohemian flair, whether objets d'art, lighting, or works of art.

Prized for its romantic scenes and daring florals, chinoiserie lends a dazzling touch, as it has since the expansion of trade routes from the Far East in the early eighteenth century. Lacquered screens, pagoda-style lanterns, and hand-painted wallpaper also bring depth and distinction to major rooms. (Reportedly, Coco Chanel displayed her collection of Coromandel screens with floral details and animal motifs in her Paris *appartement.*) Elsewhere, ceramic garden stools that double as drink tables and ginger jars adorned in blue-and-white patterns make stylish statements alone or in groups.

Anchored in a historical sensibility, the textiles and textures of Morocco (a French colony throughout most of the first half of the twentieth century) capture attention and foster a sense of intrigue. Outside influences, from Persia (modern-day Iran), with its earthenware to sunny Portugal, with hand-embroidered linens, help meld the look of North African furniture, fabrics, and handicrafts. Shapely case goods with bone inlay or mother-of-pearl are a coveted—and often imitated—export. Unvarnished brass candlesticks, fabrics in vibrant shades, and wool rugs woven using natural dyes also warm rooms.

At the opposite edge of the Mediterranean, Turkey has earned its reputation for fine cotton thanks to the long-fiber varieties native to the region. Today's vegetable-dyed kilims and carpets harken back to the height of the Ottoman Empire, as do traditional Kütahya ceramics along with intricately patterned Iznik tiles. Websites such as Etsy, online auction sales, and museum shops throughout the US offer non-travelers the opportunity to discover artifacts with multicultural roots that help master a modern mix.

Despite a troubled history at the hands of Napoleon, Venice has long held a special place in French hearts. Curvaceous rather than cut Venetian glass is a focal point in homes, whether it is a vase or glamorous lighting produced on the famed island of Murano. Versatile Venetian mirrors, meanwhile, have enchanted the French for 500 years, bringing sophistication to any space, from the salon to the bath, while bestowing global presence in homes with multicultural roots.

PREVIOUS OVERLEAF: In a nod to Louis XVI, a glazed *canapé* (settee) from Legacy Antiques, Dallas, takes pride of place in an anteroom that serves as a waiting area for an elevator. Hand-painted walls are the work of Dallas artist Carol Cravens. Pillows are Fortuny. On the Venetian island of Giudecca, behind tall iron gates with intriguing mystique, Fortuny produces rich, all-cotton fabrics with classical Italianate motifs.

OPPOSITE: Architectural grandeur juxtaposed with the sophistication of the French results in a garden room—both sumptuous and inviting—with an abundance of light. The Paris Hill lanterns are Vaughan Designs.

OPPOSITE: Tailored slipcovers with couture-inspired detailing—piping, corner pleats, and smooth rather than gathered skirts—skim settees. In 18th-century France, aristocrats often retained attendants to oversee an array of responsibilities, from maintaining upholstery to giving furnishings a fresh look with coverings echoing the season. Art propped on the mantel leans against the wall—a practice that reaches back to 17th-century England.

ABOVE: Meriting more than a passing glance is the work of the artist-in-residence, whose creativity evokes awe and envy.

LEFT: Louis XVI painted chair robed in fabric from Manuel Canovas and edged in tape.

RIGHT: Chic handblown glass bottles.

OPPOSITE: With aristocratic good looks, Louis XVI painted chairs, circa 1890, surround an Iatesta & Co. table. Handblown glass bottles vary in size and hues. Grouped together, they give the garden room a modern twist, while the antique French mirror and console add warmth. The earliest known mosaics were made in 300 BC in Mesopotamia.

For a family that often entertains, a dining room with timeless allure is central to its lifestyle. Global influences abound: A Murano chandelier from Foxglove Antiques, Atlanta, overlooks the homeowners' preexisting table. Sophisticated silk is the backdrop for contemporary art entitled *Water Stones III*—mineral pigments on Kumohada paper—by Makoto Fujimura. The 19th-century French console is from Legacy Antiques. Mirror is Venetian. Fabric from Bart Halpern covers the chairs.

ABOVE: Chairs robed in Kravet surround a table from Hickory Chair ready for playing a game or doing homework. Commode is from Dennis & Leen, custom mirror from Texas Iron & Steel. Painting is by Makoto Fujimura.

RIGHT: An area rug from Interior Resources is the foundation for a culturally sophisticated great room, where a vintage Japanese wedding kimono merits a place of honor. Although the word *kimono* rather humbly means "a thing to wear," the garment became a form of opulent dress indicating one's status is society during the Edo period, 1603–1868. Oversized L-shape sectionals don an upholstery-weight Kravet fabric in the conversation area, where Highland Court patterned and solids meet. When it comes to upholstery, turning a solid, nondirectional fabric horizontally avoids seams.

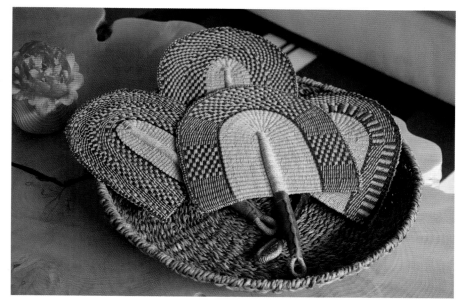

LEFT: Taking its cue from the surrounding textures, a cabana set apart from the main house plays host to a mango-root coffee table from Rotsen Furniture, Miami. Perennials stain-resistant fabrics, designed for outdoor living, cover Hernandez Upholstery. Art by Yale-educated Chris Martin makes a strong statement.

ABOVE: Humble, natural-fiber fans with leather handles, handwoven in Africa, are rife with admirable artisanship.

BELOW: Texture abounds in a drought-tolerant, mini succulent garden. The whimsical plantings are the work of Brenda Lyle.

ABOVE: A cabana bath has it all: rippled, Porcelanosa Tile that climbs the walls, a pendant from Waterworks, and Pennsylvania Flagstone flooring.

OPPOSITE: With a densely wooded area as the backdrop, a shaded area offers an escape from the Texas sun. Furniture is from RH, throw pillows from Frontgate.

Acknowledgments

Taking an idea from concept to design book is a sweeping process, a collaborative effort on the part of many people whose focus on detail is exceptional. This calls for a little name-dropping.

For opening their doors and welcoming us into their private worlds, I thank Lori and Jonny Brumley, Claudia and Dennis McClain, Penny Reid and Thomas Nolan, Chris and George Tamke, and several others.

I am also most appreciative of the distinctive way of defining style—with a chic blend of traditional and edgy—the following designers exhibited in creating the alluring, satisfying rooms that make up this book: Loren Reardon, Deborah Walker, Courtnay Tartt Elias, Cindy Witmer, and Sarah West.

Meriting a warm thank-you are those who facilitated the timely completion of new construction so our own projects could become an integral part of this book: Jim Minton, Ken Brown, Ken Brown Jr., Tim Dolan, Bob Burmiester, Rick Frisch, Barry Gannon, Dave Harrison, Harold Leidner, John Massara, Mike McCrady, Huel Pruitt, Rick Knight, and Charles Stevenson.

And there are more: John Lupoli, Stuart Beavers, Richard Watson, and Holli Watts.

Add to the above list appreciation for efforts of the following: Donna Burley, Jayne Butler, Sandra Catlett, Trinh Cao, Jody Condor, Jessica Craig, Bruno de la Croix-Vaubois, Claude Flanagan, David Flynn, Esther Gandal, Christy Gatchell, Kristen Githens, Laura Guarisco, Susan Hamilton, Tiffany Hayes, Julie Hayhurst, Christine Humbert, Kara Jones, Brian Lancaster, Sandy and Ed Linebaugh, Thomas Love, the Marroquin family —Jesus, Monica, Adrian, and Ivan—Todd Moody, Annick McNally, Patrick McNally, Allen Northington, Raymond Pittet, Penny Sanders, Margaret Shelhon, Gillian Bradshaw Smith, Janice Stuerzl, Linda Swain, Sabath Trejo, and Anna Watkins.

Without question, I want to thank friend extraordinaire Letitia Jett-Guichard. Also deserving of thanks are Tom Johnson, Delana MacLean, and Dominic Ferrara, who rallied at a moment's notice with IT support, keeping us running twenty-four seven.

Time and time again, I thank Loren Reardon for her prized design assistance. And she joins me in thanking those who assisted in installations: Kelly Phillips, Marilyn Phillips, Peggy Reardon, Brenda Lyle, Pam Holden, and Logan Jones.

As always, I have admiration and appreciation for photographer Dan Piassick, who helped make our photo shoots successful, interesting, and fun.

Add to the above list appreciation for book designers Rita Sowins and Virginia Brimhall Snow, and love for my long-time editor Madge Baird, who channels incredible energy into offering support and guidance before polishing the manuscript. Afterwards, she and her admirable team revel in the excitement of its debut and thrill in the honor when it captures sought-after bids for attention.

Finally, a big thank-you to my husband—and the family who brighten our lives. Without their understanding, this project would not be. And *merci par avance* to you, the reader, for so kindly welcoming my fourteenth design book, *French Refreshed,* into your home.

Directory

INTERIOR DESIGNERS

Courtnay Tartt Elias
Creative Tonic Design
750 Bering Drive, # 115
Houston, Texas 77057
Phone: 713.533.9000
www.creativetonicdesign.com

Betty Lou Phillips, ASID
Interiors by BLP
4200 Saint Johns Drive
Dallas, Texas 75205
Phone: 214.599.0191
www.bettylouphillips.com

Deborah Walker, ASID
Deborah Walker & Associates
154 Glass Street, # 108
Dallas, Texas 75207
Phone: 214.521.9637
www.deborahwalker.com

Cindy Witmer
Cindy Witmer Designs
1403 Whispering Pines Drive
Houston, Texas 77055
Phone: 713.278.1919
www.cindywitmerdesigns.com

ARCHITECTURAL CONSULTANT

Sarah West
Sarah West & Associates
5667 Lynbrook Drive
Houston, Texas 77056
Phone: 713.417.6714

ART ADVISOR

Helen Varola
Helen Varola Advisory
Casale Monferrato, Italy
Phone: 39.328.8765743
www.helenvarola.com

ARCHITECTS

Larry E. Boerder
Larry E. Boerder Architects
4809 Cole Avenue, #250
Dallas, TX 75205
Phone: 214.559.2285
www.larryboerder.com

Robert Dame
Robert Dame Designs
7322 Southwest Freeway # 1550
Houston, Texas 77074
Phone: 713.270.8225
www.robertdamedesign.com

Richard Drummond Davis
Richard Drummond Davis Architects
2124 Farrington Street
Dallas, Texas 75207
Phone: 214.521.8763
www.rddavisarchitect.com

J. Wilson Fuqua
J. Wilson Fuqua & Associates Architects
3618 Fairmount Street
Dallas, Texas 75219
Phone: 214.528.4663
www.wilsonfuqua.com

Jeffrey Weller
Summit Architecture PA
125 Main Street
Highlands, North Carolina 28741
Phone: 828.526.0328
www. summitarchitecturepa.com

DESIGNER PHOTOGRAPHIC CREDITS

Betty Lou Phillips: 8, 10–11, 12, 13, 14–15, 16, 17, 18, 19, 20–21, 22, 23, 24, 25, 26–27, 28, 29, 30, 31, 32–33, 34, 35, 36, 37, 38–39, 40, 41, 42–43, 44–45, 46–47, 48, 49, 50–51, 52, 53, 54, 55, 56, 57, 58, 59, 60, 61, 62, 63, 64, 65, 66, 67, 122, 125, 126–127, 128, 129, 130, 131, 132, 133, 134–135, 136, 137, 138–139, 140, 141, 142, 143, 144, 145, 146, 147, 148–149, 150, 151, 152, 153, 154–155, 156, 157, 158, 159, 160, 161, 162–163, 164, 165, 166–167, 168, 169, 170, 171, 172, 173, 174–175, 176-177, 178, 179, 180–181, 182, 183, 184, 185.

Deborah Walker: Front Jacket, Title Page, Contents, 68, 70–71, 72–73, 74–75, 76, 77, 78, 79, 80–81, 82, 83, 84, 85, 86, 87, 88, 91, 92, 94–95, 96, 97, 98-99, 100, 101, 102–103, 104, 105, 106, 107, 108, 109, 110, 111, 112, 113, 114, 115, 116–117, 118–119, 120, 121, 220, 223, 224, 225, 226, 227, 228-229, 230–231, 232–233, 234–235, Back Jacket.

Cindy Witmer and Courtnay Elias: 186, 188–189, 190, 191, 192–193, 194, 195, 196, 197, 198–199, 200, 201, 202, 203, 204, 205, 206–207, 208–209, 210, 211, 212–213, 214–215, 216–217, 218, 219.

ARCHITECTURAL CONSULTANT PHOTOGRAPHIC CREDITS

Sarah West: 186, 188–189, 190, 191, 192–193, 194, 195, 196, 197, 198–199, 200, 201, 202, 203, 204, 205, 206–207, 208–209, 210, 211, 212–213, 214–215, 216–217, 218, 219.

ART CONSULTANT
PHOTOGRAPHIC CREDITS

Helen Varola: Title Page, Contents, 92, 94–95, 96, 98–99, 100, 102-103, 107.

ARCHITECTURAL
PHOTOGRAPHIC CREDITS

Larry E. Boerder: 8, 12, 13, 14–15, 16, 17, 19, 20–21, 22, 23, 24, 25, 26–27, 28, 29, 30, 31, 32–33, 34, 35, 36, 37, 38–39, 40, 41, 42–43, 44–45, 46–47, 48, 49, 52, 53, 54, 55, 56, 57, 58, 59, 60, 61, 62, 63, 65, 66, 67, 138–139, 140, 141, 142, 143, 144, 145, 147, 180–181, 183, 185.

Robert Dame: 186, 188–189, 190, 192–193, 194, 195, 196–197, 198–199, 200, 201, 202, 203, 204, 205, 206, 207, 208–209, 210, 211, 212–213, 214–215, 216–217, 218, 219.

Richard Drummond Davis: Front Jacket, Title Page, Contents, 68, 70–71, 72–73, 74–75, 76, 77, 78, 79, 80–81, 82, 83, 84, 85, 86, 87, 88, 91, 92, 94–95, 96, 98–99, 100, 101, 102–103, 104, 105, 106, 107, 108, 109, 110, 111, 112, 113, 114, 115, 116–117, 118–119, 120, 121, Back Jacket.

J. Wilson Fuqua: 220, 223, 224, 225, 226, 227, 228–229, 230–231, 232–233, 234–235.

Jeffrey Weller: 122, 125, 126–127, 128, 129, 131, 133, 134–135, 136, 137, 138–139, 142, 143, 144, 145, 147, 148–149, 150, 151, 152, 153, 154–155, 156, 157, 158, 159, 160, 161, 162–163, 164, 165, 166–167, 168, 169, 170, 171, 172, 174–175, 176–177, 178, 179, 180–181, 183, 184, 185.

PHOTOGRAPHY CREDITS

All images are by Dan Piassick except author's portrait by Jin Kim, Dallas.

First Edition
23 22 21 20 19   3 2 1

Text © 2019 Betty Lou Phillips
Photographs © 2019 Dan Piassick

Published by
Gibbs Smith
P.O. Box 667
Layton, Utah 84041

1.800.835.4993 orders
www.gibbs-smith.com
Designed by Rita Sowins, Sowins Design
Pages produced by Virginia Brimhall Snow
Printed and bound in China

Gibbs Smith books are printed on either recycled, 100%
post-consumer waste, FSC-certified papers or on paper produced from sustainable PEFC-certified forest/controlled wood
source. Learn more at www.pefc.org.

Library of Congress Cataloging-in-Publication Data

Names: Phillips, Betty Lou, author.
Title: French refreshed / Betty Lou Phillips.
Description: First edition. | Layton, Utah : Gibbs Smith,
[2019]
Identifiers: LCCN 2018059064 | ISBN 9781423650942
(hardcover)
Subjects: LCSH: Interior decoration--United States--French
influences. |
   Decoration and ornament--United States--French influences.
Classification: LCC NK2049.A1 P475 2019 | DDC 747.0944-
-dc23
LC record available at https://lccn.loc.gov/2018059064

ON THE JACKET FRONT: A romantic palette is the framework for stylish living. Sofa fabric by Great Plains; antique Louis XVI chair covered in Coraggio mohair velvet; midcentury coffee table from Jan Showers.

ON THE JACKET BACK: Black and white marble and hand-forged wrought iron unite to create a dramatic vaulted foyer with contemporary polish.

TITLE PAGE: An open-back settee and sofas look up to Murano glass leaf pendants from Galerie Glustin, Paris. Area rug is from Stark Carpet. A signed and numbered Cy Twombly mixed-media lithograph hangs over the fireplace. Oil on canvas, 72 by 72 inches, with integrated, shimmering crystalline is the work of New York–based Margaret Evangeline.

PAGE 4: An entry with black-and-white marble inlay doubles as an art gallery. Cascading from above is a statement-making necklace of oversized, handblown Murano beads by lauded French artist Jean-Michel Othoniel, who recently created fountains for Versailles and whose works have been commissioned by Chanel, Louis Vuitton, and Cartier. Nearby is a brass triangulation chair designed by internationally acclaimed Zhang Zhoujie, a pioneer in the realm of digital creativity.

PAGE 237: The Mitchell Gold + Bob Williams table shuns classic lines for a strong, clean shape, while the chairs further the contemporary look of the dining area. Artwork is by Dennis McClain.

PAGE 239: RH Gallery daringly modern, low-slung Parisian sofas float in space. Unadorned windows and exposed HVAC piping visually raises the ceiling, complements the color scheme, and plays a major role in the setting's appeal.